Auto Racing
Life in the Fast Lane

capstone
classroom

BTR Zone (Bridge to Reading) is published by Capstone Classroom,
1710 Roe Crest Drive, North Mankato, Minnesota 56003
www.capstoneclassroom.com

Copyright © 2013 by Capstone Classroom, a division of Capstone. All rights reserved. No part of this publication may be reproduced in whole or in part, or stored in a retrieval system, or transmitted in any form or by any means, electronic, mechanical, photocopying, recording, or otherwise, without written permission of the publisher.

ISBN: 978-1-62521-046-3

Editorial Credits
Mandy Robbins, editor; Kazuko Collins, layout artist; Eric Gohl, media researcher

Photo Credits
AP Photo: David Graham, cover; Corbis: Bettmann, 7, 28, 29, epa/Khaled Elfiqi, 40–41, Icon SMI/Robin Alam, 26–27, NewSport/Walter G Arce, 17; Newscom: ZUMA Press/Action Press/XPB, 42; Shutterstock: Action Sports Photography, 4, 8, 12, 14–15, 18–19, 21, AMA, 30, Art Konovalov, 38–39, BBurcham, 22, carroteater, 24–25, Derek Yegan, 10–11, Kosarev Alexander, 36, Max Earey, 32–33, Rob Wilson, 34

Design Elements: Shutterstock

About the Cover
NASCAR driver Tony Stewart wins a race at Daytona International Speedway.

The publisher does not endorse products whose logos may appear on objects in images in this book.

Printed in the United States of America in North Mankato, Minnesota.
012013   007111BTR

TABLE OF CONTENTS

CHAPTER 1
Speed Thrills!........................... 5

CHAPTER 2
NASCAR................................ 13

CHAPTER 3
Indy Cars............................... 23

CHAPTER 4
Sports Car Racing..................... 31

CHAPTER 5
Rally Racing 37

Indy 500 Trivia........................ 42
Read More............................. 44
Internet Sites 44
Glossary of Text Features 45
Glossary................................ 46
Index................................... 48

Carl Edwards speeds around a turn during a 2010 NASCAR race.

CHAPTER 1

Speed Thrills!

Imagine driving down the road at 200 miles (322 kilometers) per hour. Your steering wheel is shaking. There is a curve ahead. Look out! All of the cars on the road are just as fast. They try to pass you. This would be scary. For race car drivers, it is a normal day. They love the speed and action. They look for the thrills. Race car drivers want to win.

Some people like to go fast. They also like to compete. Racing began when cars were **invented**. People wanted to test these new machines. They were curious to see how fast they could go. People also wanted to test themselves. They wanted to try out their driving skills. It was time to race!

invent · to think up or create something new

The first American auto race took place in the city of Chicago, Illinois. It was November 28, 1895. The **course** was about 54 miles (87 km) long. There were only six race cars. Brothers Frank and Charles Duryea won. It took them 10 hours and 23 minutes to finish. Newspaper reporters wrote about the race. This helped raise interest in cars. Auto racing became a sport that would continue to grow. Today there are many kinds of race cars. They race on oval tracks and twisty roads. They are all FAST!

How fast were they driving in that first race? Duryea drove about 5.3 miles (8.5 km) per hour. Today race cars go much faster. Some can travel more than 300 miles (483 km) per hour.

The Duryea brothers drove through thick snow to win the first American auto race.

course · the route of a race

Soon after the first race, cars were improved. They got faster. Different kinds of races began. This meant people needed different kinds of racing cars. The wheels changed. Engines changed. Even driving skills began to change. Now it takes a team to manage each car in a race. This team is called a pit crew.

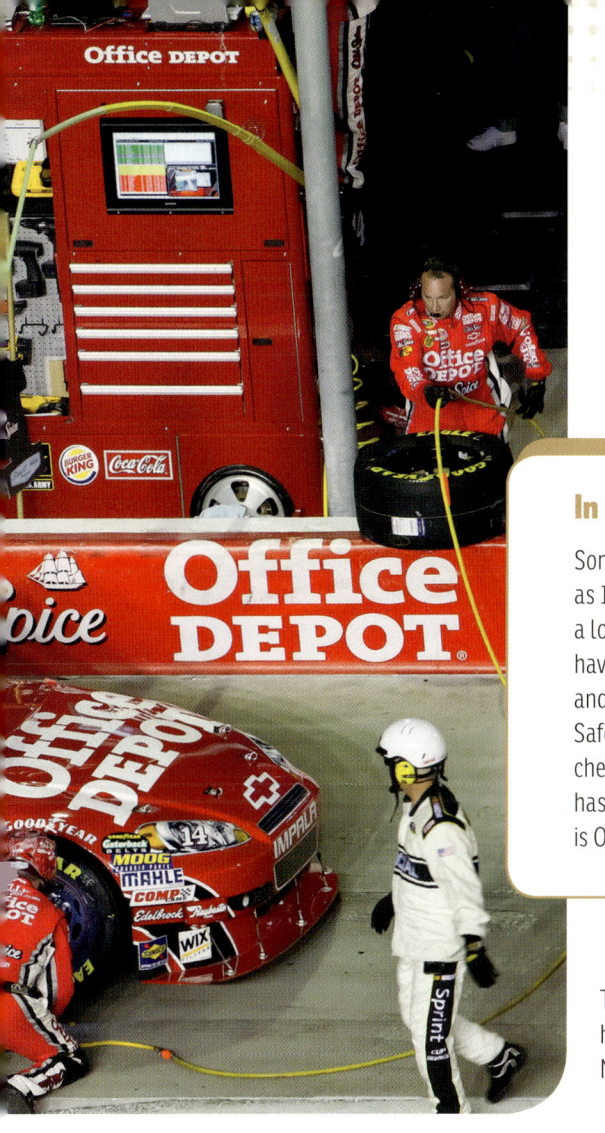

In the Pits

Some pit crews have as many as 10 members. They have a lot of work to do. They all have different jobs. Fuel, tires, and wires have to be checked. Safety features have to be checked. Of course, someone has to make sure the driver is OK!

Tony Stewart's pit crew is hard at work during a 2010 NASCAR race.

Auto racing has millions of fans. It is watched all around the world. There are more kinds of races than ever before. Men and women take part in the sport. They perform as drivers or as crew members. Each racing team can earn millions of dollars. The sport has come a long way since that first race.

Drag Racing

Drag racing is another kind of race. Drag racers drive superfast cars, such as top-fuel dragsters and funny cars. Their engines are designed to make them go as fast as possible. Drivers paint their cars bright colors. Drag racers spend a lot of time working on their cars. Winning can mean money and trophies.

drag race · a race in which two cars begin at a standstill and drive in a straight line at high speeds for a short distance

A top-fuel dragster speeds to victory.

Drag races are very short. Only two cars race at one time. When the light turns green … they go! They try to go superfast right away. They drive in a straight line. The race lasts only a few seconds. The winner races again. The loser is done. Races continue until one car is left. That car is the winner.

CHAPTER 2

NASCAR

National Association for Stock Car Auto Racing (NASCAR) championships are a big deal. They are like the Super Bowl of auto racing. Millions of people follow NASCAR.

Why is NASCAR so exciting? One reason is the cars. They look similar to cars you see on the road. But these cars are different. A lot of work has been done to make them ready to race. They have special engines. They also have safety features such as roll cages. Fans like to see these powerful cars roar around the track. The speed is exciting. Most people don't drive this fast!

Want more reasons? NASCAR fans watch the races on TV. They also buy tickets and watch in person. Auto racing is a lot like other sporting events. Fans buy food and gifts. They also cheer for their favorite drivers. They are with other people who love auto racing. Tracks like the Indianapolis Motor Speedway hold more than 250,000 fans.

Stock car drivers prepare for a 2009 NASCAR race.

Fans pack the stands of the Bristol Motor Speedway for a NASCAR race.

How popular is NASCAR racing? Fans are everywhere! The group holds more than 1,500 races in the countries of the United States and Canada. They also have smaller races in the countries of Japan, Mexico, and Australia. People in over 150 countries watch NASCAR on TV!

Right on Track

The NASCAR track is an oval. Each oval is a little different. They are not all the exact same length or shape. There are also many rules in NASCAR. Drivers have rules to follow. So do their teams. Even the cars have rules. Driving fast can be dangerous. Rules make sure that everyone is as safe as possible. They also make sure each race is fair.

In the United States, NASCAR has the second highest TV **ratings**, or popularity, for sports events. Most of the top 20 one-day sports events are NASCAR races. NASCAR fans spend a lot of money on the sport.

NASCAR holds many special events. The Sprint Cup **Series** crowns a champion every year. So does the Nationwide Series. The Daytona 500 is part of the Sprint Cup Series. It takes place in the state of Florida. The race is 500 miles (805 km) long! More than 200,000 fans attend this event. The Nationwide 300 is also a big race for the Nationwide Series. This course is 300 miles (483 km) long. It is held the day before the Daytona 500. It takes hard work to win a NASCAR race. Prizes include awards, such as trophies, and money.

rating · a score that reflects the popularity of something
series · a number of things coming one after another

Daytona 500, 2012

The NASCAR Sprint Cup Series is the top level of competition. It is also the most popular series. It earns the most money. The 2011 winner was Tony Stewart. He started driving early. He got his first go-kart in 1978. He was 7 years old. By 1999 Stewart was a new NASCAR driver. He won **rookie** of the year his first year racing. He went on to win many races.

Tony Stewart sits in the driver's seat.

rookie · a person who is playing for the first year in a sport

19

Jimmie Johnson is another great Sprint Cup driver. He won the championship five times in a row. He was the winner from 2006 through 2010.

Over the years there have been other great champions. Fans know and love winners like Richard Petty, Dale Earnhardt Sr., and Jeff Gordon. Each driver had what it took to win. They combined speed and skill to race to victory.

Driver Safety

Sadly, some NASCAR drivers have been killed while racing. Each time, NASCAR puts stronger safety measures in place. These measures include special clothing for the drivers. They also include special **devices** to support the head and neck. Safety will always be an important issue in racing.

Jimmie Johnson cheers after winning a 2010 race.

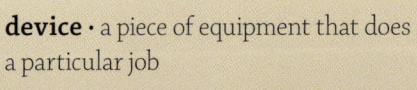
device · a piece of equipment that does a particular job

Several racers speed around the track during a 2011 Grand Prix race.

cockpit

CHAPTER 3

Indy Cars

Indy auto racing is also very popular. People like it because the cars are **unique**. Indy cars are not like NASCAR cars. The placement of the wheels is different. An Indy car is an open wheel race car. This means the wheels are outside of the car's body. There is only one seat in an Indy car. NASCAR vehicles have two seats. Indy cars have more **technology** than other race cars. The entire car is built like an upside-down wing. This helps the car stick to the track even at high speeds.

The seats in an Indy car make them unique. The **cockpit** is very small. Only the driver can fit. It is a very tight space. Indy cars do not have roofs. The driver's head sticks out of the car. Imagine sticking your head out of a sunroof at more than 200 miles (322 km) per hour! It's not safe. But Indy car drivers do it all the time.

> **unique** · one of a kind
> **technology** · the use of science to do practical things, such as designing complex machines
> **cockpit** · the place where a driver sits in a car

Marco Andretti speeds around the track during the 2010 Indy 500.

The inside of an Indy car is unique too. Most other cars have engines in front of the driver. The engine of an Indy car is behind the driver. The engine moves the rear wheels. This movement helps push the car forward. These engines help the cars move very fast. Indy racing is among the fastest in the world. The cars reach a speed of 220 miles (354 km) per hour.

wings

Many Indy cars have wings at the front and rear. They are not flying wings. The wings help keep drivers safe. Without them, the cars might lift off the road. The wings help keep the cars **stable**. At such high speeds, Indy cars need some extra help. The wings help them stay on the road.

stable · not easily moved

25

Drivers circle the track before the 2012 Indy 500.

The Indianapolis 500 is the most famous Indy car race. It is part of the Championship Series. The Indy 500 has been called the greatest event in auto racing. As many as 400,000 fans attend every year. The cars race at the Indianapolis Motor Speedway. This track is an oval shape. Drivers have to go around the track 200 times. They drive 500 miles (805 km) in a single race.

Indy cars need a lot of power. **Horsepower** (hp) is a measurement of how much work a car can do. It also describes how fast a car can do the work. Indy cars need a lot of horsepower. It takes practice and talent to handle such a powerful engine. Indy drivers are among the best.

horsepower · a unit for measuring an engine's power

A. J. Foyt with one of his many racing trophies

Indy racing has had many famous drivers. Two of the most famous are Mario Andretti and A. J. Foyt. They were not just great Indy winners. They also won NASCAR's biggest event, the Daytona 500. Andretti was born in 1940. He worked with his twin brother to build his first car. He drove in his first race in 1959. Andretti went on to race and win for 41 more years. Foyt was born in 1935. He decided to be a race car driver before he went to elementary school. Today he owns his own Indy racing team. Foyt **retired** as a driver in 1993.

Women in Racing

For many years, women drivers were not allowed to race. In 1977 Janet Guthrie became the first female to race in the Indianapolis 500. She also was the first female in the Daytona 500. She did that the same year. Since then, there have been nine female drivers in major races.

Sarah Fisher has competed more than any other female driver. She has raced nine times. Danica Patrick is the only female to lead laps during a race. She led 19 laps in the 2005 Indy 500. She led 10 laps in the 2011 Indy 500. Her third place finish in 2009 is the best finish for a woman.

Janet Guthrie prepares for a 1979 Indy car race.

retire · to give up work usually because of a person's age

Grand Touring sports cars speed around a track in a 2009 race.

CHAPTER 4

Sports Car Racing

Sports car racing is also popular. Many **advanced**, cutting-edge cars are made. They are similar to NASCAR models.

Sports cars made for racing come in different styles. There are two main kinds. One kind is sports **prototypes**. These cars are newly designed cars. The other kind is Grand Touring cars. Sports prototypes are two-seat racing cars. These cars are very advanced. They go really fast. Grand Touring cars look like cars you see on the road. Inside, they are different. They need special features for racing. These include extra padding and nets. Cars that are not used for racing do not need these features.

> **advanced** · being able to do more and work better than others of its kind
>
> **prototype** · the first version of an invention that tests an idea to see if it will work

Most sports car races are long races. They can last up to 24 hours. Drivers want their cars to be fast. They also want their cars to last for the whole race. Sometimes a driver gets tired. Then a new driver takes over. This makes car racing like a team sport. There are also team **managers**, or leaders. They are very involved in the races. Some managers are almost as famous as the drivers.

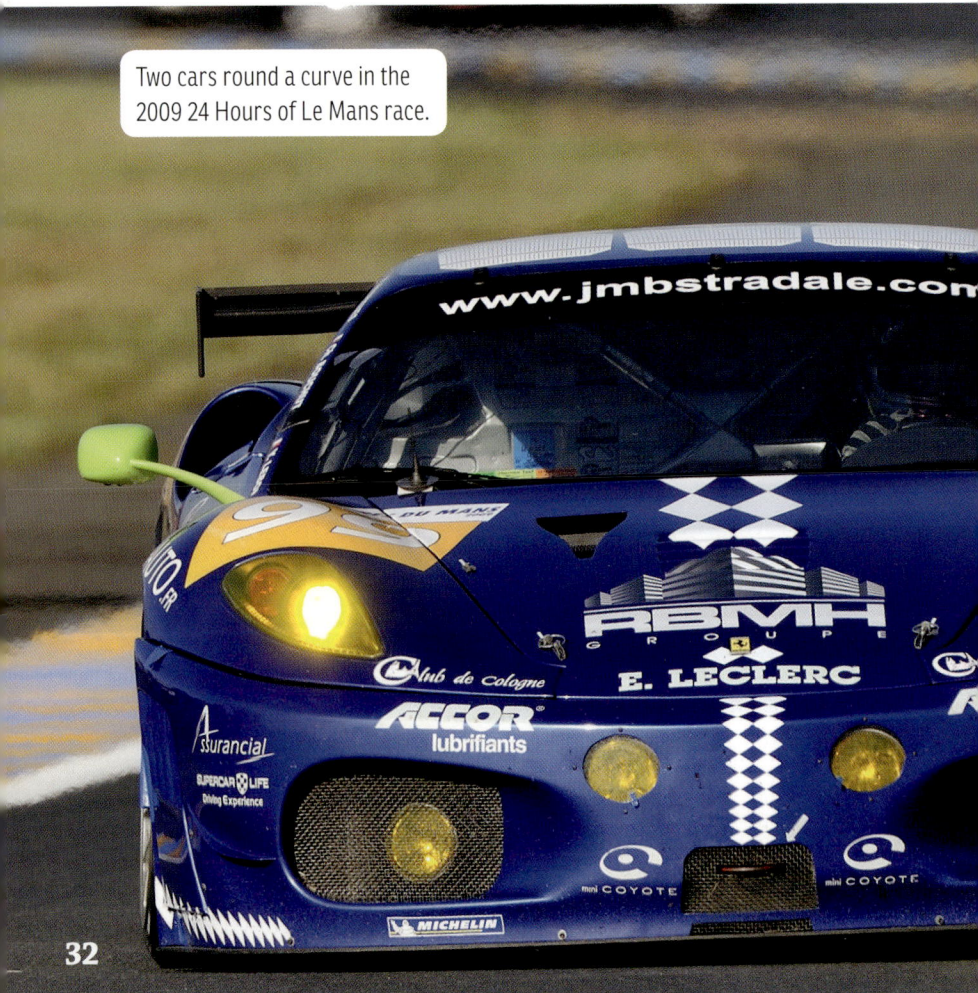

Two cars round a curve in the 2009 24 Hours of Le Mans race.

The World Sportscar Championship is a series of races. Some races are more famous than others. One of the most famous is the 24 Hours of Le Mans. It is held in the country of France. The American Le Mans Series is a similar race. It was created in 1999. The 24 Hours of Le Mans has been around since 1923. After all these years, people still love these races.

manager • a person in charge of a group

33

A 2012 BMW is displayed at a car show in Jacksonville, Florida.

24 Hours of Le Mans

The 24 Hours of Le Mans is the world's oldest sports car race. It has been held every year since 1923. It takes place near the town of Le Mans, France. Race teams have to be fast for 24 hours. Drivers switch almost every two hours. Today it is a rule that three drivers share each vehicle.

You don't have to be a race car driver to own a sports car. Some sports cars can be bought at car **dealerships**. But sports cars cost a lot of money. A sports car can cost more than $100,000! You pay more for a fast engine and extra horsepower. Many companies that make sports cars are well known. The companies have become famous. They include BMW, Porsche, and others. Many people would like to own a car made by one of these companies. Owning one is a sign that the car is well made—and fast!

dealership · a place where items such as cars are sold

35

A rally driver soars over a hill during a 2008 rally race.

CHAPTER 5

Rally Racing

Are there any auto races with regular cars? Yes, there are **rally races**! Rally racing is different than Indy and NASCAR racing. Rally cars are not driven on an oval track. They start at one point on a road or highway. They end at another. Each race has different steps called **stages**. There is also a co-driver. Instead of one person inside, there are two. The co-driver can tell the driver about the road. He or she can tell if there are bumps or ice ahead. In some races, the fastest driver wins. In other races, the driver closest to a set time wins.

rally race • a timed race from one point to the other that is run in stages

stage • a step in a process

A rally car kicks up dust during a 2010 rally race.

There are two main types of rally racing. One is called a **stage rally**. Stage rallies are the **professional** races. Racers earn money. The cars travel on roads closed off to other traffic. Stage rallies can be on gravel or mountain roads. There might be ice and snow or desert sand on the road. The drivers like different roads. It is a good way to test their cars. It also tests their driving skills.

stage rally • a rally race held on a route that is closed off to other traffic

The other type of rally racing is called a **road rally**. Road rallies were the first kind of rally race. They are held on highways. The highways are open to normal traffic. Road rallies are often long races. The winner has to finish closest to a set time. There are not many road rally races anymore. They can be dangerous to other drivers.

professional · a person who makes money by doing an activity that other people might do without pay
road rally · a rally race held on highways with normal traffic

Andreas Schulz (left) and Khalifa Al-Muitawei (right) wave after winning the 2012 Pharaons Rally race.

Rally drivers buy their cars at stores called car dealerships. Then they get them race ready. They make the engines more powerful. They paint the cars however they want. When their cars are ready ... off they go!

40

Rally Racing

What if you were riding in a car in the city? Imagine being surrounded by speeding cars. It would be scary. Rally car drivers like the speed. Of course, only trained drivers would be in a race. It takes years of practice to learn how to drive a rally car.

Rallying is a very popular sport. People can join car clubs. Club members learn about rally cars. These clubs often hold their own races. Driver and co-driver practice together. Teamwork is important for winning rally races.

Indy 500 Trivia

The Indy 500 has been called the "greatest spectacle in racing." The race is 500 miles (805 km) around a track. Once the race starts, it's roaring action from start to finish.

Indianapolis Motor Speedway

Q. Why 500 miles (805 km)?

A. The race was first held in 1911. Owners thought most people would like a race lasting about seven hours. A distance of 500 miles (805 km) was chosen.

Q. Who is the youngest winner of the Indianapolis 500? Who was the oldest?

A. Troy Ruttman was 22 years, 80 days old. He won on May 30, 1952. Al Unser was 47 years, 360 days old. He won on May 24, 1987.

Q. Who was the first to drive an official lap at 200 miles (322 km) per hour?

A. Tom Sneva drove just over 200 miles (322 km) per hour on May 14, 1977.

Q. Why do the winners celebrate by drinking milk?

A. Three-time winner Louis Meyer drank buttermilk on hot days. A picture of him drinking milk became popular. Drinking milk is now a long tradition.

Read More

Gigliotti, Jim. *Teamwork at the Track*. The World of NASCAR. Mankato, Minn.: Child's World, 2009.

McCollum, Sean. *Racecars: The Ins and Outs of Stock Cars, Dragsters, and Open-Wheelers*. RPM. Mankato, Minn.: Capstone Press, 2010.

Murray, Robb. *A Daredevil's Guide to Car Racing*. Daredevil's Guides. North Mankato, Minn.: Capstone Press, 2013.

Internet Sites

FactHound offers a safe, fun way to find Internet sites related to this book. All of the sites on FactHound have been researched by our staff.

Here's all you do:
Visit *www.facthound.com*
Type in this code: 9781625210463

Check out projects, games and lots more at *www.capstonekids.com*

Glossary of Text Features

Text Feature	How to Use It
Caption: A word or group of words shown with a picture or illustration	Read a caption to understand information that may not be in the text.
Diagram: A drawing that shows or explains something	Examine a diagram to understand steps in a process, how something is made, or the parts of something.
Glossary: List of key terms with their meanings	Look up key terms in the glossary to find their meanings and to get a better understanding of the topic of the text.
Index: Alphabetical list of key terms, names, and topics in a text with their page numbers	Use the index to find pages that contain information you are looking for.
Map: A drawing that represents a place, such as a country or city	Use a map to understand relative locations and determine where events took place.
Photograph or Illustration: Visuals that are created by cameras or drawn	Examine photographs and illustrations to better understand ideas in the text that might be unclear.
Subhead: Word or group of words that divides the text into sections and tells the main idea of a section	Use subheads to locate information in the text and understand how a text is organized.
Table: Represents data in a small space	Examine a table to understand data or to compare information in the text.
Table of Contents: List of the major parts of the book and their page numbers	Use a table of contents to locate general information in the text and see how the topics are organized.
Text Box: A box in the text that provides extra information about a topic	Read a text box to understand interesting or important information.
Text Style: Bold, color, or italic words in the text	Pay attention to bold, italic, and color words to figure out which words in the text are important.
Timeline: Shows events in the order in which they occurred	Use a timeline to understand the order in which events occurred or how one event led to another.

Glossary

advanced (ad-VANST) • more fully developed than others of its kind

cockpit (KOK-pit) • the place where a driver sits in a car

course (CORSS) • the route of a race

dealership (DE-luhr-ship) • a place where items such as cars are sold

device (di-VISSE) • a piece of equipment that does a particular job

drag race (DRAG RAYSS) • a race in which two cars begin at a standstill and drive in a straight line at high speeds for a short distance

engine (EN-juhn) • a machine in which fuel burns to provide power

horsepower (HORSS-pou-ur) • a unit for measuring an engine's power

invent (in-VENT) • to think up and create something new

manager (MAN-uh-jur) • a person in charge of a group

professional (pruh-FESH-uh-nuhl) • a person who makes money by doing an activity that other people might do without pay

prototype (PROH-tuh-tipe) • the first version of an invention that tests an idea to see if it will work

rally race (RAL-ee RAYSS) • a timed race from one point to the other that is run in stages

rating (RAY-ting) • a score that reflects the popularity of something

retire (ri-TIRE) • to give up work usually because of a person's age

road rally (ROHD RAL-ee) • a rally race held on highways with normal traffic

rookie (RUK-ee) • a person who is playing for the first year on a team

series (SIHR-eez) • a number of things coming one after another

stable (STAY-buhl) • not easily moved

stage (STAYJ) • a step in a process

stage rally (STAYJ RAL-ee) • a rally race held on a route that is closed off to other traffic

technology (tek-NOL-uh-jee) • the use of science to do practical things, such as designing complex machines

unique (yoo-NEEK) • one of a kind

Index

24 Hours of Le Mans, 33, 34

Andretti, Mario, 28

Daytona 500, 16, 28, 29
drag racing, 10–11

Earnhardt, Dale Sr., 20
engines, 8, 10, 13, 24, 27, 35, 40

fans, 9, 13, 14, 16, 26
Foyt, A. J., 28

Gordon, Jeff, 20
Grand Touring cars, 31

horsepower, 27, 35

Indianapolis 500, 26, 29, 42–43
Indianapolis Motor Speedway, 13, 26, 42–43
Indy cars, 23–29

Johnson, Jimmie, 20

NASCAR, 13–20, 23, 31
Nationwide Series, 16

Petty, Richard, 20
pit crews, 8–9

rally cars, 37–41
rules, 15, 34

safety, 13, 15, 20, 25
Sprint Cup Series, 16, 18, 20
Stewart, Tony, 18

48